Advance Praise

"I love this book! Sarah Jane takes us with her in her clear, step by step path to growing herself and her relationships. I felt like I was having coffee with a new best friend while reading it. It is intimate, effective, fun and beautiful!"

      —Dack Quigley, First Class Facilitator, Owner of The New Game, LLC, Mentor & Friend to Sarah Jane

"Sarah puts her heart and soul out there for this enlightening and heartfelt book. While I was not sure I could relate to being "broken" in my marriage, her ideas and positive outlook are relatable in the sense that even a good marriage could be better. The questions she asks and the path she follows is inspiring for any person on a journey for more happiness. She kept me interested by including influences from relatable aspects of her life and included stories and advice from friends that were from all walks of life. My attention was grabbed when she posed a grand idea of just asking for what we want. While so simple, Sarah took the idea and ran with it, and turned it into an everyday way of getting what we need. The book left me with small tasks to make my life easier and my relationship better."

—Robyn Potts

"The book was fantastic! Sarah was extremely personable, raw, transparent, and motivational. I was able to relate to so many experiences in this book. The book was a breath of fresh air! I cannot wait to put BEAUTIFUL into action in my relationship!"

—Michelle Case

"*From Broken to Beautiful* is an exquisitely written account of Sarah Jane Patton's awakening out of the nightmare of a distressed marriage into an empowered loving partnership with her husband. Patton's gentle goodness tackles the dark issues of abandonment, betrayal, and hopelessness with a guiding light that is accessible to all who choose to use it. Her ultimate message, told in clear, heartfelt, down-to-earth and easy to follow steps is that you can transform your marriage-and your life. It takes work. It takes a willingness. But it is possible. Her life is proof. Important read for anyone who is ready to liberate themselves from the shackles of frustration, despair or hopelessness - as well as for anyone looking to upgrade the happiness factor in their lives."

—Robin Winn

From Broken to Beautiful

9 SECRETS THAT WILL
TRANSFORM YOUR MARRIAGE

FROM
BROKEN
TO
beautiful

SARAH JANE PATTON

NEW YORK

LONDON • NASHVILLE • MELBOURNE • VANCOUVER

From Broken to Beautiful

9 Secrets That Will Transform Your Marriage

Published in New York, New York, by Morgan James Publishing in partnership with Difference Press. Morgan James is a trademark of Morgan James, LLC. www.MorganJamesPublishing.com

ISBN 9781631950155 paperback
ISBN 9781631950162 eBook
ISBN 9781631952104 audiobook
Library of Congress Control Number: 2020931919

Cover Design Concept:
Jennifer Stimson

Cover Design by:
Jonathan Lewis

Interior Design by:
Christopher Kirk
www.GFSstudio.com

Editor:
Emily Tuttle

Book Coaching:
The Author Incubator

Author Photo:
Shane Michael

Morgan James is a proud partner of Habitat for Humanity Peninsula and Greater Williamsburg. Partners in building since 2006.

Get involved today! Visit
MorganJamesPublishing.com/giving-back

This book is dedicated to Dr. Richard Otto Olson, Jr.
In your memory, I dedicate this book to you. Thank you for
loving me unconditionally, always believing in me and for
sharing your generous heart. I am eternally grateful for you.

—

Table of Contents

Chapter 1:

How Did I Get Here

As I reflect on my life over the past several years, I can't help but think about all that I have been through in my marriage and all the other silent, suffering women dealing with the same anguish I once had. I remember my mind being consumed by thoughts of how to set myself free of the misery I was living in and how I could flee from the toxicity. Trying to decipher what risk I was willing to take made me physically sick. Sleepless nights of tossing and turning became normal and my brain felt like a tornado inside my head. I so desperately wanted to figure out how to bring the love and spark back to my marriage and I cried endless tears, as no solution ever seemed to surface.

Maybe you've spent countless hours trying to figure out what your next move is. I bounced back and forth from trying to figure out how to make the marriage work to planning my exit strategy. One day I would have my mind made up and the next, I would sob for even considering the plan I had come up with. Perhaps you feel moody and overwhelmed by your thoughts and every little thing he does seems to increase your negative thoughts of him. Something that in the past would have rolled off your shoulders has now become a battle with a vengeance. Your resentment and resistance to him is growing like a fertilized weed. It takes off quickly and furiously, spreading in every area of your relationship. Trust me, I get it. My anxiety took over my life, fear consumed me, and blank stares wondering how to escape the pain seemed endless. My husband and I fought about everything and the distance seemed to increase daily. Everyday tasks seemed to be impossible to complete and it was becoming increasingly obvious that I was withdrawing from my inner circle of friends and family. Social outings began to fade into the past.

I had already had one failed marriage, and I was beating myself up at the thought of facing this again. I couldn't understand how I was repeating what I had already lived through. Perhaps you did what I did and asked yourself, "How did we even get here?" I never had an answer, and typically, I was looking to blame him for where we were and could only see his shortcomings. I would lay in bed next to him, loving and hating him simultaneously, then ask myself, "How is this even possible? How can you love someone and hate them at the same time?" I spent many days staying in my pajamas with no desire to shower or even brush my teeth. I stayed in bed as much as I could and wanted to hide from my truth. On days I had to face the world, I would get up and put a smile on my face attempting to keep my secret from my family and friends.

However, the dark cloud of my unhappy marriage followed me throughout the day, and the storm never seemed to dissipate. Taking care of my children became a burden and my fear of how things would affect them only increased the pain and anxiety. Every breath I took became a chore. But, when you remove the hate, anger, and frustration, you want the marriage to work because you still feel so much love for him. Maybe that's what gives you a

4 | **FROM BROKEN TO** *beautiful*

glimmer of hope. You are probably clinging to that hope and feel like you're hanging over a cliff struggling for your dear life. I know —I've been there.

Chapter 2:

Where I Discovered My Truth

It was a gloomy spring morning and I was sitting in my favorite chair in the living room, sipping on my coffee and gazing out the window. Thoughts of leaving my husband and planning my exit strategy were racing through my mind. Feelings of failure at another marriage and frightened at the thought of splitting our family up were starting to consume me more and more each day. I sat in that chair, looking out the window at the beautiful property we had just purchased six months prior. To an outsider, our life looked amazing, but the truth was we were barely communicating. Each day seemed like I knew him less than I once did. I wanted so desperately to make it work and certainly didn't want anyone to know we weren't living the happily ever after we had dreamed of. Our differences seemed to be pulling us apart and keeping us from living the life we both once imagined having.

We had been in a relationship for nearly five years and had gotten married six months prior. I needed to have major surgery and didn't have insurance at the time. Since we had already planned to get married and a wedding date already set, we decided to secretly tie the knot and still celebrate with family and friends the following September. I sat there trying to understand how we had quickly taken a wrong turn in our relationship, and felt sick to my stomach at the thought of walking away from it all. The surgery was more invasive than we had anticipated and everything surrounding the situation seemed to pull us apart even more. After much contemplation, we decided to postpone the wedding. It was easy to tell everyone it was because of my health issues, but we both knew the truth; we were drifting apart.

I have always tried to be someone who could remain positive and try to see the bright side to things. But at this point in my life, I felt like negativity was holding me hostage and dooming thoughts were consuming my mind. I slipped into a deep depression and was doing everything I could to make sure my secret wasn't exposed to the outside world. I didn't want to get out of bed, I was withdrawing socially, and toxic behavior began radiating from within me.

Today, as I write this, I am so grateful for the journey I have been on and to be where I am at in this moment. The tribulations I faced are what led to my greatest victories and if I had to do it over again, I most definitely would, just to be where I am right now. My experience is a perfect example to show others facing a similar situation that there is hope. My husband and I have traveled to a place of love through unending determination. It wasn't easy, but it was worth every mountain we had to climb. I knew that I loved him enough to try and find a way to fix what felt so broken. I embarked on a mission to save my marriage. I didn't know the how. How we would overcome our differences, how we could improve our communication, how things would ever be like they once were. All I knew was that I loved him and that was enough to push me to make a change.

Hiding from the truth was almost more painful than actually going through the unpleasant experiences that lead to my troubled marriage. I have always valued my integrity, so not exposing the truth about my relationship made me feel like I was living a lie. It also felt all too familiar, as I had already been down this road after my first failed marriage of fourteen years. Feelings of shame and failure paralyzed me.

Then one day, my friend Susan called me and asked me to attend a presentation with her. We were both real estate agents and she had been looking at some new investment opportunities, frequently inviting me to attend some of these informative seminars with her. I would typically decline, mostly because she knew me so well and if I was around her, the truth about my relationship may be exposed. This time, when she called to invite me, I was so desperate to get out of the house I didn't care where we were going. I just knew I needed to get away and escape the reality I was living, so I quickly accepted her invitation.

When we arrived, I suddenly realized I was not at a real estate seminar. The people greeting the guests were overly happy and I wondered what was wrong with them. I asked myself how they could be so happy to greet people they never even met before? What exactly was this all about and why was I here? The presentation was a personal growth seminar called The First Class. Afterward, when I met Sandra, the woman who was presenting the information to this small, intimate audience, she greeted me with a huge smile and warm embrace. It should have felt weird, but for some reason, it didn't. Perhaps it was because I could feel that she was genuinely happy to meet me.

I quickly learned that she had been waiting to meet me and that Susan had been telling her about me for quite some time. I had taken in all the information that Sandra shared and was trying to sort through why she was so excited to meet me. So, because I was intrigued to know more about what she had presented, I immediately decided I wanted to attend The First Class. As Susan and Sandra celebrated my commitment to attend, it was in that moment that I realized my dear friend already knew my truth. She may not have known the specifics, but she knew me. She knew something wasn't right and she was certain this personal growth seminar would be exactly what I needed.

Desperate for change and feeling like I had nothing to lose, I informed by husband that I would be gone for a weekend to attend The First Class. When I arrived, I was happy to be there, but more than anything I was curious about what I was going to gain from attending. I sat in the front row and a man by the name of Dack Quigley introduced himself. I instantly fell in love with him. He was funny, animated, direct, and his passion for what he did beamed through him as he spoke.

This personal growth seminar, The First Class, changed my life so much that it will be frequently referenced throughout this book. I had previously been exposed to much of what Dack taught, either through prior work seminars or self-help books, and I have applied so much of what I learned in this seminar throughout my life but not consistently. From the moment it was over, I was never the same.

On the last day, there was an opportunity for people to stand up and share how their experience attending The First Class had impacted them. I stood at the front of that class knowing that when I left that day, my relationship could be salvaged, and I was confident I would get there. I shared what I had discovered about myself, where I was wrong and responsible for contributing to the contamination of my relationship. I instantly felt myself forgiving, not only my husband, but more importantly myself. I felt empowered and equipped, not only to make a change in my marriage, but to share what I learned and what I already knew with the world. I stood at the front of the room and declared that I would pursue my dream of writing a book and becoming a motivational speaker. I knew in my heart that I would have to share what would transpire as a result of my choices.

Over the next several months, I began applying nine revelations I identified to not only my marriage, but to my own personal development. My relationship began to shift immediately, and our communication improved with each new day. I was excited to get out of bed and face the day, something I hadn't felt in a really long time. I began making decisions about choosing my own happiness and felt confident that I could do anything I put my mind to.

One of the hardest things for me to embrace was that much of what I had already been taught or the things Dack had shared, my husband had known all along. Looking back, he had tried to show me so many of these amazing lessons and approaches that were from a different perception of the everyday world. I know now that not allowing myself to see what he already knew was crushing him. I had to dig really deep to uncover why I could only hear and apply it when Dack taught me, not when my husband was trying to. What I discovered was sometimes we do not open ourselves up to the ones we are closest to. As crazy as it sounds, it is easier to tell your truths to and take advice from strangers or someone we feel is more qualified than the ones we love.

Throughout this book, I will share with you real life situations I faced that allowed me to discover nine secrets that transformed my marriage from broken to beautiful. I am not going to sit here and tell you about what education I have or don't have, how I am more qualified than someone else or that I know it all, because I certainly do not. What I am going to do is be genuine, honest, and passionate about spreading the message I know so many women are in need of hearing. I have made a commitment to, not only share my message, but to walk you through each step that lead to my amazing transformation. I will openly share my personal experiences with you and expose my personal triumphs and tribulations I faced. I want to help you navigate this process and guide you to the healing and happiness you are searching for.

Chapter 3:

How to Go from Broken to Beautiful—My Nine Secrets Unveiled in a Step by Step Process

Throughout this book, we will unveil the nine secrets I discovered that transformed my marriage in a step by step process. We will walk through each step and I will guide you through the path to go from broken to *beautiful*. Below is a summary of what we will cover in each step:

B—Build Your Dream

I want to start by helping you identify what you want. Often, we don't take the time to consider what our ideal marriage looks like or what our dream come true is. We tend to focus on the negative and forget that our dreams and desires matter. I will walk you through identifying what exactly you want, help you build your dream, and create a vision for your ideal marriage.

E—Experiences Do Matter

One thing I have discovered is that our past experiences do matter and can affect how we react toward our spouse in our daily interactions. Bringing this to light will help you to understand why you and/or your husband respond the way you do and will allow you to be mindful of how past experiences may dictate our responses.

A—Ask for What You Want

In this step, I will teach you how to ask for what you want. This may sound silly; however, we often assume our spouse knows what we want, but we forget to directly ask. I will show you how to effectively communicate with your husband by asking for what you want and learning how to be direct when asking. I will also help you identify the difference between assumption and asking. This secret will become a game changer in your relationship, and I am confident about how much of an impact it will have on your relationship when it comes to communicating.

U—Understanding Your Limiting Beliefs

What is a limiting belief, you might ask? A limiting belief is something that you believe to be true and limits you from doing something. Limiting beliefs can be detrimental to your marriage. I will help you to identify what your limiting beliefs are, understand how they can be toxic to your marriage, and learn how to overcome them.

T—Take Control of Your Own Happiness

I will teach you how to choose your own happiness. This step often appears to be unreachable, however, I will walk you through a simple lesson that will change your entire perception on how to take control of your own happiness.

I—I Have to Love Myself?

As women, we tend to put everyone else first and forget about self-love. In this step I will show you how loving yourself and putting your needs first is imperative to having a healthy relationship with yourself, and how that will improve your marriage. I will also teach you that the act of self-love can often be mistaken as being selfish and help you to overcome that belief.

F—Forgiveness is a Necessity

We all know how hard it can be to forgive someone. At times, it can be even harder to forgive ourselves. I will share with you my personal experiences of some of my biggest acts of forgiveness and show you how being able to forgive can create growth and closeness to your husband.

U—Unanswered Prayers

Unanswered prayers are simply life lessons that occurred that, in the end, weren't the result you were looking for. However, it benefited you or your relationship in some way. I will walk you through some of my unanswered prayers and show you how to turn a past negative experience into a lesson learned and then welcome them with gratitude.

L—Letting Go of Fear

In this last step, I want to leave you understanding how fear can hold us back from reaching our desired happiness and dream come true. I will show you that fear is simply a feeling. I will walk you through overcoming your biggest fears and how to place belief in yourself and in your marriage.

The most important thing here is understanding what you are facing, accepting what you cannot change, and committing to creating the success you desire to achieve. I will walk you through the journey I took to attain the happiness and successful marriage I have today. Various emotions may surface as you dig deep and dive into each step. Please be assured that I will be with you through this journey, and I too felt many of the same emotions and struggles you may encounter along the way. I recommend that you take notes and journal about your own experiences, identify what emotions come up, and explore how you feel about applying the step to your life. Highlight what resonates with you most. By the time you finish reading the book, I hope you feel inspired and confident that you have what you need to make a change. You can take it a step further by reaching out to me, and I can help you along the way as you work through each step. To get information, email me at: sarahjane@lifecoachsarahjane.com.

Chapter 4:

Build Your Dream

Have you ever sat down and thought about what your ideal marriage looks like? Of course you have, because we all think about what we wish we had. Do you find that you are always focused on the negative aspects of your husband? His shortcomings? What he didn't do or how he could be better? Where he is failing as a husband, and so on? I used to make a mental note of the things that irritated me about him and all the things he did that annoyed me. I knew I loved him, but seriously, this stuff would get on my nerves. Here are some examples of things I couldn't stand:

- ❦ He chews with his mouth open. —Who does this? Didn't your mother teach you to chew with your mouth closed? Where are your manners?

- ❦ He doesn't always come home when he says he will. —I don't care that he goes out with his friends, but can't he just come home when he says he will, or at least call me when he's not going to?

- ❦ He has the need to be right. —Why does he always have to be right? I know what I am talking about!

- ❦ Holidays aren't important to him (unless it's the fourth of July). —Don't you want to see the kids open all their gifts? Don't you want to see everyone get together for the holidays?

- ❦ He leaves everything in his pockets and if I don't check before they go in the laundry, it will all get washed. —Do you realize there is $300 in your pocket? Finders keepers! Seriously, why can't he just throw his trash away?

- ❦ He knows I am on a diet, so why is he bringing me my favorite cookies? —Does he not understand that I am trying to lose weight? Is he trying to sabotage what I am doing? Is he testing my willpower? What is happening here and why isn't he being supportive?

❦ He isn't there for me. —Does he not understand that I am sad and going through a hard time right now? Why does he hate it when I cry? Why can't he just be there for me? He should know what I need, and I shouldn't have to tell him!

If you look at this list, most of it is pretty petty, but these were the things that made me crazy and that I was always focused on. It began to feel like we were fighting all the time, and the tension and conflict just seemed to get worse. After almost five years together, I started feeling like we were drifting apart. I found myself disconnecting, not wanting to spend time with him, not wanting to do the social things we once did together. And the ultimate red flag that something wasn't right—lack of physical contact. Yep, when I didn't want to hug him, cuddle anymore, or could care less about our sex life, I knew something was wrong. I can remember lying in bed hoping he didn't touch me, that he would just roll over and go to sleep. I would even pretend to snore to send the signal loud and clear—*do not touch me*. Suddenly, it slapped me in the face. Oh no, I am heading down the same road from my previous marriage!

How is this happening again? I love this man, but why does it feel like I don't know him anymore? Why are we barely communicating? I didn't know the answers; I only knew that the feeling was all too familiar, and if I didn't do something, I was going to be divorced again.

What negative things do you find yourself focusing on about your husband or marriage? Make a list of all the things that drive you crazy, or things that feel like deal breakers in your relationship. Can you identify which items are petty and which really need to be addressed, if any?

Initially, I was focused on what *my husband* could do to improve our marriage and how if *he* would just change, it would all get better and we could move on to our happily ever after. It sounded good to me, but what I discovered is that it doesn't actually work like that. After many attempts at trying to get him to make changes, I came to a conclusion. When I started to work on improving the marriage first, and he started noticing my changes, he magically started to follow my lead. If you are willing to identify some things that would make your husband happy or changes he would like to see from you, and then work on applying what you know, you will be surprised how the marriage will begin transforming into what you have been desiring.

On day two of The First Class seminar, the teacher said something that grabbed me by the shoulders and shook me to my core. He said, "To get the love you want, you must first give that love." Wait… what? So you are telling me that if I want him to love me a certain way that I have to love him that way first? I made note of it and decided I wanted to prove that teacher wrong. I thought, "There is no way this will work, this guy is crazy and clearly doesn't understand how women operate." Well, the truth is, all I did was prove him right! Let me tell you more.

Years ago, I became a Mary Kay consultant. What I loved most about the company was the positive outlook they had and the uplifting training they provided to their consultants. I was exposed to some amazing books and authors that would birth my belief in understanding the power of my mind and positive thinking. I discovered what it meant to have a vision and how to make my dreams a reality. Over the next fourteen years, I would utilize that knowledge, but not consistently. However, when I did use it, it worked every time. Not sometimes—*every time*. Over the years, I would forget and slip back into old mindsets. I wasn't consistently using the knowledge I was taught, and as a result, I would fall right back into my negative thoughts and behaviors.

As I sat through the seminar, much of what was being taught was information I had learned when I was a Mary Kay consultant. The material was very similar to many of the books I had already been exposed to years prior. I thought to myself, what if I took what I knew about how to create a vison and applied it to my marriage? If I applied the rule of loving him the way I wanted him to love me, could it create what I dreamed of having? My arms were being pulled in two different directions—one was saying yes, you know this works and you have proof by your prior success created by the vision you had set out to achieve. The other was saying, prove that teacher wrong about loving him like I want him to love me. Desperate for change and on the verge of divorce, I had nothing to lose.

I sat down and thought about what my ideal marriage looked like. It was something like this:

We are happy. We effectively communicate. He gets me! We spend quality time together and have fun again. We are great parents successfully raising our large, blended family. We have a healthy sex life and no issues with physical touch or intimacy. We are best friends again. We rarely fight and when we do, we work through our issues in a healthy manner. I can't get enough of him; he is the love of my life!

It seemed perfect and was what I dreamed of having, but was it possible? *Yes*, it was possible!

I was so focused on the negative that I couldn't see all the great things about this man I fell in love with five years ago. My thoughts were consumed by what we didn't have and looked for what was wrong. I had to find the good in him. I knew it existed or I wouldn't have married him. So, I made note of all the positive things about my husband. This is what I came up with:

- He undoubtedly loves me; he has proven it a million times over.
- He works hard and provides for our family.
- He respects me.
- He wants me to be successful.
- He is patient—quite possibly the most patient human being I have ever met!
- He is generous.
- He surprises me with my favorite cookies and candy.
- He accepts my five children from my previous marriage.
- He is intelligent.
- He unconditionally loves his family.
- He is a devoted father.

Get out the list of negative things you wrote down about your husband. Now, make a list of all the positive and loving things about him. Find every amazing quality and compare your notes. It is likely that you have more positives than negatives, and when you can step into those positives, then you are able to find gratitude for all that he is, not what he isn't. What I found works best is, after you have made the comparisons, toss the list and rewrite it to only include the positives. Review them daily, and definitely when you are having uneasy feelings about your marriage. Sometimes, we have to remind ourselves of what we have. If you want to take it a step further, which I highly recommend, start a gratitude journal. When you can acknowledge the things you are grateful for, you will begin to shift your mindset. Keeping a gratitude journal can help relieve stress, improve your sleep, and allow you to gain perspective on things. Many studies have been done on the benefits of keeping a gratitude journal. Take a moment to do a google search and see what you can find. If you want my help, feel free to email me for more information.

When I changed my focus to what I did have instead of what I didn't, the first change I noticed was how I felt about our marriage and how I felt about him. I began to feel happy instead of sad or angry, hopeful instead of despairing, confident that we could get the spark back. Most importantly, I felt the love again. I created a vision of what I wanted our marriage to be, and when I started loving him the way I wanted him to love me, things began to change immediately. When I began doing things for him, such as rubbing his back, going out of my way to grab something I know he loves, or giving him my undivided attention, he started doing the same back. I couldn't believe it. The relationship began to change and transition right away. Every day, I would envision us being happy and spending quality time together, and me feeling in love with him again. On days I felt like I didn't like him, I would consciously recite all the reasons I loved him. I knew what I wanted and applied the love reciprocation rule I was taught in that seminar, and I was blown away by the results. Dang, I proved the teacher *right*.

Do you know what you want? Is this something you have even considered or really sat down and thought about? To get what you want in your relationship, before you do anything, you must know what you want. Otherwise, there is nothing to work toward. Make a list and paint the picture of your ideal marriage. Make a list of all the things that you *do* love about your husband and apply the love reciprocation rule. Start your gratitude journal and watch your marriage that feels so broken start to transform. This is where it begins. Grab your pen and paper and start building your dream! If you need help getting started, then reach out to me and I can help you!

Chapter 5:

Experiences Do Affect You

Something I have come to learn that has truly helped me effectively communicate with my husband is that my past experiences affect how I respond to him. If we dig into our childhoods and how we were raised and reflect on past relationships and life experiences in general, we will begin to realize that we subconsciously create feelings based on these life events that cause us to respond based on what we previously experienced. Emotions are attached to the experiences and they've become imbedded in our subconscious mind. So, when similar events occur or repeat themselves, or even if the event just feels similar to something else, our subconscious mind literally takes over. Have you ever driven a car somewhere and arrived at your destination, but don't remember how you got from point A to point B? We all have. Our subconscious mind takes over and gets us to where we are going. This happens when we communicate with people and we don't even know it's occurring. It has so much control over us, yet we typically aren't even aware of it.

One day, I found myself full of anxiety about asking my husband if he cared if I was gone for a weekend. I played out the conversation in my head a million times. I thought of all the reasons he wouldn't want me to go, came up with ways to make his life easier if I was gone, and even prepared myself for the fight I just knew we were going to have. The closer I got to having the conversation, the sicker I felt. Why was I having so much anxiety over this? Why did I feel sick to my stomach? Suddenly I remembered what I had learned about having those internal programs, and the lightbulb went off. I was preparing for this conversation with my current husband based on my past experiences with my ex-husband. *What*? Yes, that is exactly what I was doing! Had my current husband ever been mad that I was gone for a weekend before? No. Had he ever told me I couldn't go or nagged me about not being there? Never. Had my ex-husband and I fought about this before? Yes, and often. It made me really think, do I do this all the time? Do I always make him pay for my past experiences?

I had to really sit back and reflect. And as I started going through several situations in my head, I realized that I made him pay for my past and it had absolutely nothing to do with him! Wow, this was awesome and awful all at the same time. It was awesome because now that I had discovered it, I could now stop and ask myself if I was feeling a certain way because it applied to the person I was actually interacting with or if it was based on a previous experience. It brought light to how my subconscious mind was working against me and then allowed me to consciously become aware of how I should respond. Once I discovered this, I was able to *consciously* think before I responded to my husband.

This would be a great time to pull out your journal and make a list of any negative experiences you have had prior to your marriage. What have your past relationships been like? Is there a chance you have made your husband pay for someone else's mistake? Please know this is very common and *do not* beat yourself up over it. The point is to acknowledge it and work toward being mindful the next time a conflict occurs. Make sure you are responding directly to what's in front of you, not something that may have occurred in your past.

What about your childhood, are there things that you went through that may unknowingly be seeping into your marriage? Again, this is so common and something most of us are not even aware of. When I discovered I was doing this to my husband, I felt terrible. However, I am so grateful I was able to work through my thoughts and become conscious of how I would respond to him in the future. This is how I became mindful, and I challenge you to dig deep and see what you can come up with. I would love to help you work through this step, and if you feel like you could use some help then send me an email to get started!

This was a life changing discovery for me and so beneficial to helping me improve my relationship with my husband. By becoming aware of my subconscious decisions based on previous experiences, I was able to understand how they were not only contaminating my relationship but affecting how I was communicating with my husband. More often than not, I wasn't even aware that I was doing this, and it seemed crazy to me that this could even happen. I began to look at how it may have affected other relationships in my life, such as with my kids, friends, and coworkers. We do this with everyone and don't even know it. They don't know it either and typically are left thinking, "What is happening?" They don't know your subconscious is running your thoughts, responses, and emotions. They also don't know that they are doing it too.

You cannot change how others respond; however, you can change how you respond. And you can bring light to those whom you are closest to by letting them in on the secret of how their past experiences may be running their responses and emotions! As you discover past experiences that may be affecting how you communicate, remember to journal them. Being able to recognize that it is happening is how you will be able to change your mindset.

Once I discovered this, I was able to talk through it with my husband. We were able to have open dialogue. Now, we are even able to ask each other if one of us may be responding based on a previous experience, or if it's really how we feel. Our communication improved drastically, and he started to understand why I may have responded to things in certain way. Discovering this can be very sensitive and bring up unexpected feelings. Approach it with caution by preparing yourself for how you may feel when you realize how your subconscious mind, developed from past experiences, may be dictating your responses. This goes deep into your core, rooted from your earliest moments. You may always have the subconscious, learned reaction initially, but if you take the time to decipher what is really happening versus what has happened, you will begin to respond more openly and effectively when communicating with your spouse.

Chapter 6:

Ask for What You Want

Why are we so afraid to ask for what we want? It's not like we don't think about how great it would be to have something or wish we had something. We think about what we want all the time, but we don't ask for it. Is it fear that holds us back? Let's face it, the worst that can happen is someone says no. How is that worse? We are afraid of hearing no. We place emotions on what we want, and the emotions are intertwined with the answer of yes or no.

I learned that in order to have successful communication in my marriage, I have to ask for what I want. This is hard to do for most people, especially if you are a passive person. I am quite the opposite of passive yet asking is still hard for me. My lesson on asking for what I want came when I least expected it. Let me explain.

I had a massive umbilical hernia that made me look nine months pregnant. After giving birth six times, the last thing I wanted was to look pregnant again! It took a toll on my self-esteem and I didn't have insurance for months after losing my job, so I just had to deal with it. My husband named the hernia Henry, to help make light of the situation. He knew how much I hated having the hernia and how self-conscious I became of my appearance. So, he did whatever he could to help me feel better about it. After nearly a year of walking around with Henry, I was finally set to have surgery.

What initially was supposed to be a laparoscopic procedure that should have been outpatient surgery turned into a major surgical procedure. The doctor told me he would have to cut me open, do the repair, and cut through my stomach muscles to release the tension and prevent a reoccurrence. This was the second time I had the hernia, but this time was much worse, and I definitely didn't want to go through it again. They told me I would be spending four days in the hospital and would be down and out for around eight to twelve weeks, with a full recovery taking up to a year. I was less than thrilled; however, I was anxious to get rid of Henry.

I went in for my surgery and things went well, all things considered. Until day two. That's when things began to crumble. I was miserable and in the worst pain I had ever experienced. I couldn't shower because I had a drain tube coming from my abdomen. I had an allergic reaction to one of the drugs, so I was covered in hives. It kept getting worse and I felt like the hospital staff wasn't listening. I couldn't go to the bathroom unassisted and it would take up to an hour to have someone help me. My husband came by early that morning to bring our daughter by to see me. Then, he dropped her off with a babysitter so he could prepare some things at home for my return.

Later that evening, I called him and asked if he was coming back to the hospital. He told me he wasn't planning on it. He informed me that he had picked up the walker and shower seat and was waiting for his cousin to come by to help carry a recliner upstairs to the living room so I would have somewhere to sit once I returned home. He told me after they were done moving the recliner, they were going to have a drink. When he told me this, I immediately lost it. I couldn't think of a time I was angrier or more hurt. He was going to have a drink when I was laid up in the hospital. We had a *huge blow* out fight that lasted for weeks.

I felt like he abandoned me at my lowest of lows. I felt like he didn't care about me and I couldn't understand why he didn't come to be with his wife at the hospital. He had been there the day before and that morning, but why was he out having a drink when I was laid up in a hospital bed? I cannot think of a time that I felt worse, not just physically, but mentally as well.

I was struggling with the fact that I wasn't going to be able to pick up our daughter for twelve weeks. She was just a year old and that's tough on a mama bear and her cub. There were other big events happening that I had to postpone or miss out on because of the recovery. I sat in my anger and emotions for days. I tried talking to him about it because I wanted to tell him how wrong he was for not being there for me. The angrier I became, the further he distanced himself from me. Yes, I was pointing the finger at him. I mean, isn't it common sense that if your wife is in the hospital, you go be with her?

Isn't it common sense to just do this? I shouldn't have to tell him to do it. *He should know…* or so I thought.

We eventually decided to move on from the disagreement because every time we talked about it we were reliving the situation and nothing good was coming from it. We both chose to agree to disagree. The truth is, I was still angry. I was still hurt. I was still bitter. I even told him I had never felt more distance between us than I did after this disagreement. I began having conversations with myself about leaving him and was plotting my exit strategy. I was saying I forgave him, but that was a lie because inside I knew I had not done so.

Fast forward several weeks to when I attended that personal growth seminar. The teacher explained that we must ask for what we want. As I listened to him explaining the lesson on this, my mind immediately went back to this situation. I pulled the teacher aside during the break and explained my situation that occurred. He looked me right in the face and said, "Did you ask him to come to the hospital?"

I replied, "Should I have to ask? Isn't that common sense?"

He firmly replied, "*No*, it's not. If you want something, you have to ask for it." He then asked me again, "Did you ask him to come to the hospital?"

I said, "No, I didn't think I needed to ask him. He should have known!"

He smiled and shook his head and went on to say, "This will be a great lesson for you in learning to ask for what you want. If you wanted him to come to the hospital you should have asked him." I was fuming. I thought this guy was nuts and that I should bail on this seminar, because he seriously just told me that I shouldn't be mad because I didn't ask?

Over the next two days, I really sat back and thought about it. I even talked to the teacher again and he asked me to relive the situation, but through my husband's perspective. I did just that. I sat back and thought about what his day was like and what might be going through his mind. This is what it looked like to me:

OK, my wife is having major surgery. She is going to be down for several weeks, so that means I am running the show at home. I will have to figure out dinner every night, figure out who will help her with the baby when I return to work, and how the kids will get to school since she won't be able to drive. Oh, I need to get the walker and the shower chair for her, so she has it when she returns. Let's see, the baby is with the sitter, so I have to pick her up tomorrow. So now would be a good time to call my cousin over to help me with the recliner. Yeah, this is going to be a long twelve weeks, but we will get through it because we always do! Her meds, I can't forget to pick those up. I better start making a list or I will forget everything!

Perhaps he was a little overwhelmed by the disruption of our normal routine and preparing to take on all tasks at hand solo. I began to soften as I looked at it from his perspective. I believe that in his mind, he had a ton to do in a short amount of time and I was being taken care of by the nurses and staff. So, when he was asked to have a drink, he probably needed it at that point. A moment to take a breath, a moment to unwind from the chaos and household disruption knowing he would not have much help over the next twelve weeks. Yeah, he wanted to go have a drink. I felt like I needed one just after thinking about it all.

As I began to reflect over the situation and what I said to him, I owned that I had never directly asked him to come to the hospital. If I had just been direct with him and said, "Will you please come be with me at the hospital? I really need you," would he have done it? I wholeheartedly believe he would have. However, I didn't ask him and therefore, he didn't come.

Now would be a great time to take a moment and ask yourself, "Do I directly ask for what I want? Or do I assume he should know?" Try to think of a time you wanted something and your husband fell short of your expectations. Were you direct in asking for what you wanted? I think my husband should know to give our daughter a bath before bed when I am not home. But, this is an assumption, and if I don't ask him directly to do it, then I can't be mad if it doesn't happen. Do I think my husband should know to refill the soap dispenser when it is empty? Of course, but again, it is an assumption. Yes, these things may feel like they are common sense, however, we cannot be mad if we do not ask. There is no better way to communicate than being direct and asking for what you want. After you ask, then you can set your expectations based on what he responds with. This is a very simple way to change how you communicate that will have such an impact on your marriage, you just wait and see! If you need some guidance and want my help, then send me an email to get started.

How often do you get mad or feel let down because someone fell short of doing something, but in reality, you never actually asked? I began to pay very close attention to this and realized how upset I was by assuming my husband should know what to do and know what I want. The truth is, *they don't know*, and *you have to ask for what you want*. This goes with everything in your life. Every relationship you have, you must ask for what you want. I promise when you sit back and begin to dig into this, you will come to the same realization. You will understand how often you expect things, but never clearly communicate what you want and therefore, can feel disappointed, or hurt, frustrated, or angry. Perhaps you felt abandoned, like I did. You cannot be mad if you do not ask. As with anything, the more you do it, the easier it gets. Your disappointments will lessen, and your communication will drastically improve by asking for what you want. Don't wait, go ask for what you want!

Chapter 7:

Understanding Your Limiting Beliefs

What is a limiting belief? A limiting belief is a belief you have about yourself or a situation based on a previous experience or feeling but has no truth or reality to its actuality. In other words, it's a lie you make up in your head based on a negative experience or feeling. These beliefs can be about yourself or other people, but the truth is, they are nonsense lies.

Here is an example of a limiting belief I formed when I was three years old. One hot summer day, I asked my mom why she never wore shorts. She told me that she didn't wear them because she was "fat" and that "fat" people don't look good in shorts. That formed a belief in myself that if you are overweight, you shouldn't wear shorts. So, when I became overweight, I stopped wearing them! Is this true, should overweight people not wear shorts? *No*, this is a ridiculous idea that I made myself believe.

Too often we do the same thing in our relationships and it usually stems from a previous experience that caused us to feel hurt or betrayed. If you are in a relationship where someone cheated on you, you might form a belief that you can't trust people. The new person didn't cause the betrayal; however, you still don't trust them because you believe it will happen to you again.

Something I learned when I was a Mary Kay consultant is "what you think, you become." If you tell yourself you will be broke, then you will be broke. If you tell yourself you are fat, then you will be fat. If you tell yourself you will be unhappy, then you will be unhappy. If you tell yourself you are lazy, then you will be lazy. This works in a positive way, too. If you tell yourself you will be financially secure, then you will be financially secure. If you tell yourself you will make healthy choices, then you will make healthy choices. If you tell yourself you will be happy, then you will be happy. If you tell yourself you are productive, then you will be productive.

Now, you are probably asking yourself, "so, all I have to do is say these things and they will happen?" Yes! What happens is you form a new, positive belief about yourself. You recite it daily, write it down, look at it, read it, say it out loud, and do this over and over again. You will rewire your brain to believe this new thought and you will naturally begin to work toward the positive outcome you are wanting to achieve. It sounds simple because it is. I have done this for years and know that it works. I also know that when I stop doing it, I fall back into the old negative belief and when I do that, it takes over quickly like a plague.

You might be asking yourself, "Well what does this have to do with my relationship?" To that I say, are you focusing on what you don't have instead of what you want? Are you reciting all the negative beliefs about your relationship as it is now? Likely you are. Remember in Chapter 1 when I was focusing on all the things I was annoyed at by my husband? My attention was completely focused on his negative behaviors and my annoyances with him. When I focused on the positive things I loved about him, my relationship began to change.

Years ago, I belonged to a moms group. Typically, once a month we would have a mom's night out. Looking back at those nights out, it seemed like a whine fest. We would all vent about our husbands and how they annoyed us or how our kids were driving us crazy. I look back on that and think about how different it would be for me to attend a night out like that now. Don't get me wrong, I loved these nights and loved the ladies I was with.

Plus, let's face it, I was the queen of the whine fest, always focusing on the negative. I was fun and likeable, but I could start a whine fest session like no other! I look back on that today and think, *If I was with some of those same women now, how different would my conversations have been.* I remember we would tend to chime in with how we felt or shared a similar experience to what was being told. We often take on other people's beliefs and don't realize we are doing it. So, I caution you: become aware of the environment you are in and don't allow yourself to get sucked into these whine fest sessions. The negative thoughts can seep into your brain without you even knowing it, if you aren't paying attention. If you can redirect the conversation to something positive, then don't be afraid to. If the people you are with don't understand, that's not your problem and hey, tell them to read this book so they can understand where you are coming from!

Most people underestimate the true power of their mind. So much of what we do and how we react is based on what the subconscious mind believes. You must consciously change your subconscious. Now would be a great time to grab your journal and make a list of your limiting beliefs. Try to come up with at least ten things you think you can't do or don't believe about yourself. Then next to it create a new belief about yourself. See the example below.

Limiting Belief	New Belief
I will never have a happy marriage.	I have a happy marriage.
I will always be overweight.	I am healthy.
I will never trust people.	I trust people.
I am not smart.	I am smart.
I don't deserve to have what I want.	I deserve to have what I want.

Remember what I said earlier? That you think, you become. If you want to have a happy, successful marriage where you can effectively communicate, then you need to start believing that you have it. So start thinking positive thoughts, believe that they are true, toss out the negative, and throw those limiting beliefs out the window!

Chapter 8:

Take Control of Your Own Happiness

Something I discovered when I went through my divorce is that happiness is a choice. Most of what we do is a choice. You can choose to go to work. You can choose to buy a new pair of shoes. You can choose to write a book. You can choose to be happy. Yes, there will always be things that disappoint us; however, we are ultimately in charge of how we feel. No one can make us feel a certain way; we choose that too. That might make some people mad, but it's the truth. I recently heard something that really resonated with the concept of choosing our own happiness, and it went something like this: All situations are neutral ground until you give them life. We can choose to get angry or sad at a situation, just as we can choose to be happy or proud about a situation. There will always be times where you choose to give a situation life by responding with a negative feeling. But, if you can grasp the concept that it is all neutral ground until you give it life, you will find yourself being happy rather than angry, sad, or frustrated.

One day, I was hosting a garage sale at my home that I was preparing to sell. I had recently moved just a mile down the road. It was a spring morning and I was very chipper, as I was about to reach a thirty-day goal I made for myself after attending that personal growth seminar. The goal was to have my house completely emptied out in thirty days so I could get it on the market to sell. I was in my happy bubble, greeting the people as they walked up to look at the things I was selling.

About three hours into the garage sale, my husband called me and asked me where the vacuum cleaners were.

I told him that they were both at the old house because I had been cleaning for the sale. I could hear the irritation in his voice as he told me he was coming down to get them. I instantly thought to myself "Uh oh, he isn't happy, but that's OK because I am in my happy bubble and I will not let him pop my bubble!" About fifteen minutes later he came to the house to retrieve the vacuum cleaners. He began complaining about why I hadn't brought them back and why the kids didn't clean the house before they left, blah blah blah. He got in his car and headed back to the new house; I was so glad he was leaving because I didn't want any part of his negative behavior. I wanted to stay in my happy bubble.

A short time later he called me and began complaining about how the house was a mess and that the kids should have cleaned it and why didn't that get done and he shouldn't have to do it on his day off when there are plenty of teenagers around to help out. They should know it needs to be done and should take the initiative to do it. Again, blah blah blah. When he was done with his ranting, I told him I had a question for him. I said, "Did you specifically ask them to clean the house?" He did everything but answer the question, so I said it again, "Did you specifically ask them to clean the house?" Then he told me that maybe it wasn't them that he was mad at, maybe it was me because I should have told them to clean the house. So, then I asked him, "Did you specifically ask me to ask the kids to clean the house?" Remember Chapter 3, ask for what you want? I was applying that rule here because I could see and hear his anger and frustration about not having a clean house, but if he never asked anyone to do it, then really he couldn't be mad at anyone but himself for not asking for what he wanted. As I began to explain this to him, it immediately turned into a fight.

Not only did I allow him to pop my bubble, but now I was mad because he was mad. Then I was mad at myself for giving him the power to steal my happiness. This was neutral ground until I gave it life. He could have stayed mad, but I could have chosen not to get mad. Obviously, that's not how it went down. By the time the garage sale was over, I was so mad at him I didn't want to go home. I had a friend who was helping me, and she suggested we go to lunch instead of home. I quickly agreed. As we were about to leave the house she said, "We aren't going to lunch. I'm taking you to meet Big Dave."

Who is Big Dave? For years, people where I live have asked me if I knew Big Dave and my answer was always the same: No, I don't know Big Dave. It had been a while since someone asked me and then I took that personal growth seminar. Come to find out, Big Dave had taken it too. The people who attend that seminar form friendships and connections, which is just one more amazing attribute of it. The friend I made when attending that seminar knew Big Dave, and she said it was time for me to meet him.

Big Dave is the owner of The Ink Spot, a well-known tattoo shop in my local town and the creator of Tattoos and Turnpikes, a documentary showing the relationship between tattoos, motorcycles, and music. He is six foot five inches tall and weighs 275 pounds. He is bald, has a long beard, typically wears overalls, and of course, he is covered in tattoos. Do not judge a book by its cover because if I had, I would have never formed a friendship with this amazing human being. Big Dave is one of the most inspirational, motivating, wisest men I may have ever met. He is very in tune with the human mind and how the brain operates in regard to our thoughts and beliefs. He understands how our experiences matter and affect what we do. He knows how our subconscious mind works. He just gets it.

My friend convinced me to tell Big Dave about the fight I just had with my husband. I proceeded to tell him what occurred. He then told me he knew how to solve the problem and asked me if I was ready to hear what he had to say. I was ready for him to lay it out there. Big Dave said to me, "Do you want to be right, or do you want to be happy?"

Huh? I replied, "But I am right, he didn't ask for what he wanted! He never specifically asked for me or the kids to clean the house, so he is wrong!"

He asked me again, "Do you want to be right, or do you want to be happy?"

I was mad and replied with, "I want to be right and happy; I want both!"

Big Dave said, "Nope, you can only choose one; which do you choose?"

"Ah, I don't want to choose! I want to be both because I know I am right."

As I stood there looking at him, he smiled big and told me that really, I just wanted to be happy and being right doesn't matter. He first told me that when I get home, I should be as nice as I possibly could. I firmly said to him, "Hold on a minute, you want me to go home and be nice to the guy that just got mad about something he had no right to be mad about?" And just like that, with his happy little grin, he nodded and said, "Yes. Do you think you can do it? Can you just take the rest of the day and kill him with kindness?" I was mad but continued to listen to what Big Dave had to say. He told me to kill my husband with kindness and then ask him if later on we could talk about what had happened. Then, when he agreed to talk about what happened, I should open the conversation with, "I want to apologize for my part in the disagreement." Then, Big Dave said, "After you say that to him, remain silent. Do not say a word until after he speaks."

Hold on. I was already beyond irritated at the thought of being nice to my husband when I got back. Now, Big Dave wanted *me* to apologize for something I didn't do? Was this guy crazy? Big Dave went on to share an experience he had with his wife, and the outcome he got when he responded to her with the advice he just gave me. Still angry and naturally resistant to doing this, I left the tattoo shop and decided I would put Big Dave's advice to the test.

For the next ten minutes in my car as I drove home, I literally had to talk myself into being nice. Every ounce of me wanted to remain mad. I definitely didn't want to be nice, much less muster up an apology that I didn't feel he deserved. I arrived at home and instantly started killing him with kindness. It felt a little fake at first, but if I am being honest, it gradually became more natural and within just a few minutes, it didn't feel like it was being forced anymore. He was a little resistant at first as well, but the nicer I was, the nicer he was. I thought to myself, "What is happening?" A short time later, I approached my husband and asked him if we could talk about the incident when he had time and that it didn't have to be now, it could be later. He instantly responded that he didn't want to talk now and that he was leaving for the night and we could chat the next day. I kindly responded in my happy, perky voice with, "Sure, that will be perfect!"

The next morning, we were getting ready for a birthday outing for a close friend. I could already feel a difference in both of our moods, but I was really curious to see how he was going to respond once I brought up the incident again. I said, "Hey babe, can we talk about what happened yesterday?"

Before another word could come out of my mouth he said, "Yes, but first I want to apologize for being mad about the house not being cleaned. You were right, I didn't ask, and I was really just frustrated that I finally had a day off work, and I didn't feel like spending the day cleaning. I thought about what you have been doing these past few weeks to get the house ready to sell and preparing for the garage sale and I wasn't giving you enough credit for what you have been doing." Umm, what just happened? Did he just apologize to me?

All I could say was, "I accept your apology and I apologize for my part in it." Did I really have a part? Well, I could have chosen not to give it life, to not get mad, and to remain happy. Whether the apology was necessary or not, I still gave it. Big Dave didn't prepare me for him to apologize first, so I responded with what felt right. I have since experienced other occurrences like this one, and there have been times when I apologized first and then remained silent. Every time, he apologizes too. Sometimes it leads into an in-depth conversation and other times that is the end of it, but never has it gone back to fighting again. Do you know why? Because I choose not to, and I choose to be happy over being right!

I learned long ago that happiness is a choice, but Big Dave took it to another level for me. I am beyond grateful for this lesson because it truly has made such a positive impact on my marriage and my relationship with my husband. I no longer care so much about being right because ultimately it doesn't matter and being happy is better than being right. Don't get me wrong, I love to be right, but I would rather be happy! I have applied this lesson of happiness in my marriage over and over again since Big Dave taught it to me. Can you think of a time you could have applied this rule to your marriage, and can you see how the outcome may have been different? Are you willing to be happy over being right? I challenge you to practice this and watch the transformation unfold. It works, I promise it does, and if you believe that it will work, it will work! You have to take control of your own happiness, so go choose it!

Chapter 9:

I Have to Love Myself?

By definition, self-love is regard for one's own well-being and happiness. But what exactly does that mean to you? What does it mean to love yourself? To me, the idea of loving myself seemed selfish. I was always taught to love my kids, love my parents, and in general, love others first. The truth is, you must love yourself before you can truly love anyone else. As I set out on this journey to make changes in my life, self-love was one thing that I really had to work hard at. It didn't come naturally, it felt weird and selfish and wrong to me in many ways. For a long time, I misunderstood what self-love was to me. But what I found out is that self-love isn't taking bubble baths, getting a mani or pedi, or having a day at the spa. Yes, those are ways to love yourself, but the mental and psychological part of self-love goes so much deeper.

As I began to learn more and start practicing self-love, I started to see a change in my relationship with my husband. When I started taking care of my own needs before taking care of everyone else's, I not only saw a shift in how I felt about myself, but it was easier to help all those important people I have in my life. I began reciting my new beliefs to myself daily, otherwise known as positive affirmations. Here are examples of things I would say:

- ❦ I am beautiful
- ❦ I am successful
- ❦ I am an amazing mother
- ❦ I am a great wife
- ❦ I am patient
- ❦ I am kind
- ❦ I am generous
- ❦ I am courageous

❦ I am confident
❦ I am healthy
❦ I am determined

In the beginning, I would randomly take time to recite these self-affirmations throughout the day, but as I progressed, I decided to make it more routine to create consistency. I also was introduced to meditating, which was very foreign to me at first. If I am being honest, it felt awkward to do it. But, when I researched what meditation was all about and how to do it, I found out how beneficial it truly is to your health and well-being. It is proven to reduce stress and anxiety, and that was something I definitely needed help with. I also heard my friends raving about how much they loved it, so I decided to give it a try.

A short time after I began meditating, I decided to create a morning routine where I would combine meditation and my positive affirmations along with visualizing how I wanted my day to go. I would wake up and before I did anything, I would put my earbuds in and take fifteen minutes to meditate. This was the best time for me to do it because I could fit it in before anyone in the house was awake and therefore, avoid interruptions and distractions.

Then, I would get in the shower and I would visualize how I wanted my day to go. I would visualize myself being happy and create a successful day in my mind. Once I got out of the shower, I would turn on YouTube and play positive affirmations while I was getting ready. So, as I was doing my hair and makeup, I would not only listen to, but repeat the affirmations. It became a personal goal to do this at least four times a week. The more I did it, the better I felt. I paid attention to how I was feeling in general, and on days that I forgot to do this routine I definitely felt more stressed than on the days I did do it.

Immediately, my husband noticed a change in my mood and as a result, he began to be more affectionate toward me. I noticed that the more I loved myself the more he loved me. It was mind-blowing to me how something so simple could change the whole environment of our relationship. Our sex life was never terrible, however, before I started practicing self-love, the frequency had decreased. But it became amazing after I started loving myself. Being happy and taking care of myself first allowed me to love everyone else in my life in a totally different way.

There is more to loving yourself than just saying positive affirmations and meditating. Here are some more examples of ways to practice self-love:

❦ **Establish boundaries in your relationships—** When I started establishing boundaries in all my relationships, it allowed me to keep those at bay who may otherwise bring toxicity to my day. If it meant setting time limits on how much we interacted, then that's what I did. Maybe I got off a phone call after fifteen minutes instead of listening to someone complain for an hour. By doing this, I was loving myself by establishing a boundary that would keep their toxicity from seeping into my own feelings. Can you think of anyone you could set boundaries with? Make a list of who you can set boundaries with and describe how setting the boundaries will bring you more peace in your life.

❦ **Forgive yourself and others—** I had to let go of the past and forgive those who hurt me. The day I left that personal growth seminar, I made the choice to walk out of that room and leave all my baggage behind. This is loving myself because all that baggage I had been holding onto had only created negative feelings and a whole lot of resentment. It kept me in the state of being a victim, and if I am a victim, I will not move forward. I had to love myself enough to let go of it. It was a choice and it feeds into the idea of also choosing your own happiness. Is there anyone you need to forgive? Journal about any resentments you are hanging on to and see if you can forgive them. (I will also elaborate more on forgiveness in the next chapter.)

❦ **Hold your integrity high** —How am I loving myself by maintaining integrity? Integrity is something that has always been very important to me, so this one came very easily. If you hold yourself accountable to being a person of your word, then not only can other people trust you, you can trust yourself! If you can't trust yourself, then you can't love yourself. If I couldn't hold up an agreement I made with myself or someone else, then I would acknowledge it and own my faults. To love yourself you have to be honest and a person of your word! Can you think of a time someone didn't hold their word with you? Journal about your experience and how it made you feel. What about a time you didn't hold your word to someone? How did you feel about yourself by not holding your word?

❦ **Be with yourself** —This is where those bubble baths, manis and pedis and spa days come into play where you can take time to be with yourself. Maybe you like to read or go see a play. Find a hobby or activity that you love and treat yourself to these simple pleasures in life. The time you spend with yourself is a great time to reflect on the gratitude you have for everything in your life. When you spend time with yourself and are grateful for what you have, then you are loving yourself. What are some things you love to do? How would you feel if you were able to set aside time for yourself? Grow your self-confidence. What is more attractive to your husband than his wife having self-confidence? Not much! Most men *love* a confident woman and find it sexy. My husband loves when I can take charge of a situation or walk into a room knowing I feel comfortable in my own skin. This didn't come easy to me in the beginning, but the more I believed I was confident, the more confident I became. Be sure of who you are and by growing your relationship with yourself, you will naturally increase your self-confidence. Self-confidence is simply a state of mind, and anyone can master having it. Know your strengths. Make a list of what you are good at and what you are passionate about. How do you feel about these things? Your answer should be: *I feel confident!*

🌱 **Other ways to practice self-love:**

- 🌿 Take a walk or exercise
- 🌿 Indulge in essential oils
- 🌿 Take a bubble bath
- 🌿 Read a book
- 🌿 Enjoy a glass of wine or sip on your favorite coffee/tea
- 🌿 Go have lunch with a friend

The most important part of loving yourself is finding the time to make it happen. Trust me, I have a large family, work hard, and could tell you a million reasons why I don't have time for me. But I choose to do it by making it a priority and becoming a master time bender. Maybe you have to wake up a little earlier or stay up a little later to fit everything in. Or maybe you learn to multitask by saying the positive affirmations while you get ready in the morning or on your drive to work, but you can find the time if really want to.

You may be wondering, how exactly does having self-love benefit my marriage? *Choosing self-love helps to remove feelings of insecurities and jealousy which often become toxic to your marriage!* When you love yourself, your husband can fully love you. The greatest part about loving yourself is that you are creating your standards for your self-worth, which is a valuation of what you deserve to have. You deserve to be happy and you deserve to have everything your heart desires. You have to create your own happiness over relying on your husband to give you happiness, and you must know what your self-worth is. Only *you* are in charge of yourself and when you love yourself, your husband will become attracted to the happiness and love that radiates within you. It is really hard to be negative toward someone who is always happy and loving. He may even seem annoyed in the beginning, but happiness is contagious. You will naturally attract your man to you, and he won't be able to get enough of you! Start loving yourself and brace yourself for how your relationship is about to transform!

Chapter 10:

Forgiveness Is a Necessity

I have learned over the years that forgiveness is something many of us struggle with, including myself. To fully achieve inner growth, it is essential to master the art of forgiveness. Forgiveness is an emotional feeling that is achieved by releasing whatever caused an unpleasant feeling or a hurt triggered by someone's actions or words.

Not long ago, I felt very betrayed by a close family friend of mine. What I can tell you is that, aside from being hurt,

I was beyond bitter and angry. This person went to great lengths to make sure she didn't pay back money that was owed to me, so far that she hired an attorney and accused me of extortion. This did not sit well with me, mostly because she was challenging my integrity, something I hold to a high standard and truly value. I knew undoubtedly that I was right, and still to this day, I am unable to comprehend what in her mind made her believe that her version was true —I had so much documentation to back me up. I was having a very difficult time forgiving her.

I received a letter from her attorney, but I was so upset that I had to sit on it for a few days just to be able to speak about it. I was explaining to my friend, Natasha, what had occurred, shared all my facts that backed up what I knew was right, and started plotting out what my response would be and how I would handle it. When I finished speaking, she looked at me and said, "Let me ask you a question. Do you want to be right, or do you want to be happy?" Yeah, remember Chapter 8? Take control of your own happiness. It just slapped me in the face! I screamed! I was so mad when she called me out on it. However, I learned this life lesson already and I knew the answer without even hesitating. I wanted to be happy.

In order to forgive her and to reach happiness, I had to make a choice: did I want to stay in the state of being a victim? Think about the following: How would staying there serve me? How does society reward me by staying a victim? It rewards us in many ways, such as giving us the attention we want. Maybe we win a lawsuit or gain some other type of compensation. The list can go on and on. The important question is: how does this serve me from a psychological standpoint? The truth is, it doesn't. If you stay a victim, negative energy surrounds you and can often consume your thoughts. The emotions eventually spill into your relationships and absolutely will contaminate your marriage. Then, you start making those you love most pay for something that really has nothing to do with them. It is vital to your marriage to master the art of forgiveness, or you risk tainting your relationship with the negative outcomes that result in hanging on to resentment.

We often feel that we want to get revenge on the person or people who hurt us. However, I learned that revenge is like holding on to a hot coal. While you're standing there waiting to throw it on someone, you are the one who is getting burned. This analogy was taught in that personal growth seminar I attended and was life changing for me. I sat back and thought about what I could do to prove my integrity and prove that she was wrong. And yes, I felt like I wanted to get revenge on her for smearing my name in the mud. Especially when it felt so undeserved and that she was challenging my integrity, something so dear to me. I had to realize that I was the one getting burned by holding onto the hot coal while trying to figure out what my next move was. Ultimately, I had to chuck it in the suck-it bucket and move on. My suck-it bucket is where I toss the stuff I have to release before the poisonous emotions take over my soul.

What most people do not understand is that when you hold on to the resentment attached to the act that caused you pain, you are the one who truly continues to suffer. You do not have to tell someone face to face that you forgive them. You only have to say it to yourself. Yes, there are definitely times where you should say it to someone, however, it is not always necessary. Sometimes, the person we need to forgive isn't even alive or sometimes they don't even know they have created the act that caused you hurt or pain. This close family friend has no idea that I have forgiven her. That was for me, so I could release any negative emotion attached to the feelings that were born from her actions.

What I found even harder than being able to forgive someone else was being able to forgive myself. I have made many mistakes throughout my life and have beat myself up over the things I have done. Afterall, we are our own worst critics and we often give more grace to strangers than we do ourselves.

My first marriage lasted nearly fourteen years, and I had five amazing children with my ex-husband. I felt like I had failed my children when I decided to divorce their dad. I carried a ton of guilt for many years. I carried anger toward him, as well as with myself. The first few years after the divorce were some of my toughest times as a woman and a mother. There was so much animosity between my ex-husband and me. We tolerated one another for the sake of the kids, however, we avoided seeing each other as much as possible. It is tough, trust me I know! It takes a conscious effort to overcome the unpleasant feelings that go along with having an ex. But the end result makes it worth it!

Today, our relationship is much different. We co-parent our kids on a level that seems unusual to the outside world. We can sit next to each other at our son's baseball game and enjoy a conversation with each other. We have taken our kids on vacation together, celebrated birthdays with one another, and it's not uncommon for my daughter with my current husband to tag along with my ex-husband on a family outing with the kids. People often turn their heads or ask if it is weird or awkward to maintain such a normal relationship with him. No, it's not weird or awkward for me at all, it just seems like that to those observing it who don't know any better.

The relationship I have with my ex-husband is a display of what true forgiveness looks like. In order to have established this type of relationship with him, I not only had to forgive him. I also had to forgive myself. Once I was able to release those feelings, I was set free from of any emotion that once paralyzed me or held me hostage. It truly was a very liberating feeling to let go of it.

Forgiveness is so important in a marriage. There is no such thing as a perfect relationship and there will be times where you have to forgive your spouse and forgive yourself. Mastering the act of forgiveness is a choice, just as choosing to be happy is a choice. Holding onto the hurt only keeps yourself from growing and it can easily contaminate your marriage. As with the other things I mention in this book, it may be hard to do at first, but with time it gets easier. A good friend of mine who I will call the "forgiveness fairy" taught me that being able to forgive means you are releasing any judgement on the other person and you're able to fully accept them and the situation as it is. To reach the success you are trying to achieve in your marriage, it is imperative that you find the ability within yourself to forgive yourself and others. Forgiveness is a necessity to achieve a successful marriage!

Chapter 11:

Unanswered Prayers

When people would tell me that everything happens for a reason, I used to think it was such a cliché. Only as my mindset and how I looked at life began to shift did I realized how true this really was. Sometimes we don't know why something happens, but we must accept it for what it is. If we can't change the outcome, then there is no sense in dwelling on what should have been. It does not serve us in a positive way. Really, it is a reminder that we have to be able to fully accept something just as it is.

As I began to reflect on circumstances in my life that were less than favorable or pleasant, I began to realize there were lessons I learned from those experiences. Rather, it was a realization, or even a door that opened as a result of the outcome becoming different than I had planned or anticipated. They became my unanswered prayers. Take my situation with Henry the hernia as an example.

One day, I was looking at the scar on my stomach and I instantly smiled. The very first thought that came to my mind was how grateful I was. Yes, I said grateful. I was grateful because, as a result of all that I went through with my husband during that time in my life, I was able to learn how to ask for what I want. Had I not gone through that experience, one that at the time seemed like one of the worst in my life, I would not have been able to strengthen my marriage and grow with my husband as a couple. It was painful to go through, of course physically, but the mental part was more painful. I was planning my exit strategy and had that not happened, I may have ended up divorced again. I see this as an unanswered prayer. Look how much more I gained from the situation and how strong my relationship became. Being able to work through that with my husband brought us back to life.

There are many other things I have encountered in my life that make me feel like this. It may not appear to me right away, but most of the time I can find the unanswered prayer that comes from an outcome that was unplanned or that I had anticipated differently. Can you think of an unpleasant experience you have had in your life and find something good that came from it? What about a disagreement you had with your husband? Can you sort through the situation and find something you learned about him or yourself as a result of going through that experience? Finding unanswered prayers is a little tougher than some of the other steps I've walked you through. Trust me that they are there. I challenge you to dig deep to find them. Journal your thoughts and feelings as you dive into this exercise. If you need help you can email me!

Losing my corporate job was one of the hardest things I have been through. It took me two years to find the positive in having that happen in my life. I had to find forgiveness in myself and the people I had worked for. I was living as a victim for a very long time after losing my job. I felt resentment and definitely set out to get retributive justice on the company I had worked for. I thought after settling a lawsuit against them that I would feel better. Newsflash, I *did not*!

Losing my job while I was pregnant was devastating. I went from a nice corporate income to being on food stamps and Medicaid. I look back on that now and can tell you that I am so grateful it happened. However, it took a toll on my relationship, for sure. I was depressed. I felt worthless, I hated life, and the bitterness that resided inside of me would make you want jump ship if you saw me coming. Not only did I allow my emotions to run me, but I made others pay for what I felt. We dump on the ones we are closest to because they are our safety net. But there comes a time when they don't want to be dumped on anymore, and if we aren't careful, we may very well end up divorced and alone. Today I can say I am grateful that I lost my job. I not only learned so much about myself, but I am now pursuing my dream. This became another unanswered prayer because had I not lost my job, I may have never written this book. I may not have ever attended that personal growth seminar, and I may not have ever learned how to truly forgive myself or someone else.

I challenge you to try and find the positive in things that may appear to be negative or things that go unplanned. Learn and grow from the experiences and place value in the unanswered prayer that may come from the unexpected. Journal some of your negative experiences in your marriage and identify what positive things you can bring from the situation. Sometimes they don't appear right away but reflect back on the situation and see if you can find an unanswered prayer. Always remember that when you remain in a negative mindset, you are unable to be fully open to receiving anything that is positive.

When you can find the positive in a negative experience that has occurred, it becomes an unanswered prayer because you learned something from it. These situations often lead to some of our greatest accomplishments and biggest wins, especially when it comes to our relationships with people or in our marriages. Can you think of a time something didn't go as planned, but in the end you were grateful because, as a result, you got an outcome that you didn't see coming? What was it? How did you feel when it happened? How do you feel now? These are miracles sent by God into the universe. They are your unanswered prayers.

Chapter 12:

Letting Go of Fear

I love fear—said no one ever! Fear is an emotion based on a belief that something bad will happen. Back when I was a Mary Kay sales director, someone told me that fear stands for False Evidence Appearing Real. This has stuck with me for over fourteen years. When I feel like I am facing fear, I remember what I learned and remind myself that I don't have anything to back up why I should fear something.

We tend to focus on the negative feelings or thoughts that are a result of fear. Fear can cause anxiety, stress, insomnia, and many other symptoms. Fear often holds us back from pursuing our dreams. Fear is uncomfortable. When fear takes over, it can be paralyzing. Fear often dictates our actions. Through my journey with fear, I found three key steps to help sort through it:

- ❦ Acknowledge that fear has arrived—You have to first recognize that it has showed up. Write down what your fear is and be as specific as possible.
- ❦ Identify what's causing the fear—Determine what is causing your fear and write it down. This is typically a limiting belief you have.
- ❦ Tell fear to leave—This may sound silly to you, but trust me on this, you have to tell fear to leave. You can write fear a letter, or you can stand in front of the mirror and demand the fear go away. Then, write down a list of new beliefs that reverse the fear and hang them where you can read them daily.

Fear usually means something is at risk. Are you fearful that your marriage will end in divorce? If you are always focusing on the fear of something instead of what could be, then you can't ever move forward or grow. I found that some of my arguments with my husband were stemming from a symptom or feeling that was resulting from fear. More often than not, I had no idea that's what was happening. I started paying close attention to how I was feeling when I found myself getting frustrated or mad at him. I noticed that many times I was sitting in some other feeling based on the fear of something that really had nothing to do with him.

Fear is always with us and there really is no such thing as being fearless. Even being aware of what fear is and developing an understanding on how to overcome it doesn't mean it won't try to sneak in, especially when you least expect it. When I sat down to write this chapter, ironically, I found myself sitting in fear once again. So much so that I started doubting that I should even write this chapter or include it at all. I started telling myself I wasn't qualified enough to write it, which, by the way, is a perfect example of having a limiting belief. Then I started feeling like I was a phony for sitting in fear when I am trying to teach you how to overcome it. How does that make any sense? I had to walk through the steps I just taught you first. Then I thought, why not share what I just went through? It's a perfect example of how fear never goes away, you just learn to manage it. So, here's my story about how I was sitting in fear just as I was about to write this chapter.

As an entrepreneur, I have been a go-getter my whole life. I have spent much of my time looking for new opportunities to become more successful. I used to be the queen of starting something big and not finishing. As I set out to write this book, a dream I have had for over twenty years, I wanted to quit a million times. I have several things I am working on right now, aside from the book, all of which are some pretty big risk-taking opportunities. Many times, over the past several months, I have wanted to quit, but this time, unlike all the other times, I continued to push forward and here I was writing this book and pursuing some huge dreams.

When I woke up the morning this chapter was written, I didn't feel the excitement about writing like I had all the days prior. *What is wrong?* I thought to myself. *Why am I not skipping through the house singing, "it's a great day to be alive," like I had the day before? Why aren't I greeting everyone that morning with my annoyingly chipper voice? Why am I so irritated with the kids about not taking care of the chores I had assigned the day prior?* I mean, this was routine, with as many kids that I have. I found myself being snappy and feeling agitated at every little thing. If something could irritate me, it did.

I called my husband and interrupted his workday so I could vent about my frustrations. The more he talked, the angrier I got. By the time I hung up, unbeknownst to him, I was mad at him and hoped he wasn't going to call me back, not even to see if my day was better because I was irritated. I walked through the house allowing minor things that hadn't been taken care of the day before to increasingly annoy me. I could physically feel the tension in my body surge. I even snapped at my assistant, who was undeserving. I knew I wasn't feeling right and something was definitely wrong. I began cleaning the house because my mental state was not ready to be writing a chapter of a book!

The night before, I had finished three chapters. My goal was to complete four, but I was tired, and it was late. So, instead of writing I decided to work on a homework assignment that was due the next day. Part of the assignment was to watch a forty-minute video on launching my new book. The video was very informative and truly explained my options for what was next after I finish writing this book. Once I finished the video, I realized I had a big decision to make. Thousands of thoughts were racing through my mind, but the one that kept coming back was, "what if it doesn't work?" I decided to go to bed because I really didn't want to think, not even for another minute.

So there I was, sitting in my frustration, and as I was pulling the laundry out, I was trying to decipher why I was so agitated, when suddenly it hit me like a ton of bricks. I knew what was wrong with me! I was sitting in the state of fear! *That's what is happening*, I thought to myself. I instantly broke down crying. Not little tears and sniffles, a full-on, ugly, sobbing cry.

I immediately went to my assistant and told her what was wrong. "It's fear! *I am afraid!*"

She asked me, "What are you afraid of?"

I replied, "I am afraid to launch my book. I am afraid of success. I am afraid to invest in my success. *I am just afraid!* How am I supposed to write a chapter on fear right now, when I am sitting in it?"

She smiled at me and said, "What better time to write about it?" She grabbed her phone and said, "Here, watch this."

I sat at the kitchen table and watched the video she pulled up. It was of Big Dave—remember the tattoo artist I mentioned earlier in the book? He was sharing his own experience of fear and explaining that we have to stay out of the hows and stay in the whys. Focusing on why we are doing something is so much more important than how we will do it. He said to ask yourself, "Why is what I am doing important?"

He then said if you focus on the why, then you can fall in love with it. If you fall in love with it, then your belief and your state of being changes. The universe will match that and will give you more of what you want.

But if you are caught up in the how, fear sets in, and negative thoughts will consume you. If you change your belief, then your actions and your potential change, which increases your belief, and the fear will disappear. If you don't have belief, then your actions don't produce your desired results. Your potential is lowered, and the belief begins to disappear. Big Dave is a wise man. His message left me asking myself, "Do I want to believe that I can successfully write a book, or do I want the fear that I can't write the book?" And that was a no brainer!

A short time later, my husband returned home from work. He sat down at the kitchen table with my assistant and me, and I proceeded to share my feelings with him about the fear I was facing. He said to me, "Sarah Jane, let go of the fear and bring back the confidence you have been whirling around in for days. Keep writing the book and believing in what you are doing. I believe in you and I fully support you. You got this!" Of course, I began to sob again and quickly got up and embraced him with a tight hug. Do you see how much fear can interfere with how we communicate in our relationships without even knowing it?

This applies to all relationships, not just your spouse, and it is quick to take over! Fear holds us back all too often and we give it way too much power. In that personal growth seminar, I learned that if you aren't uncomfortable, then you aren't growing. And if you aren't growing then you are decaying. To gain the greatest success, whether it be a relationship, a career, or a huge goal, you must conquer fear, embrace being uncomfortable, and push through even when you feel like giving up. The more uncomfortable you are, the greater success you will have. I'll be really honest with you: I have never been more uncomfortable than I have since I took that personal growth seminar, because it pushed me to pursue my dreams. The fear I felt is what makes people give up! I had to walk myself through the three steps I mentioned above —I had to acknowledge it was happening, identify what was causing it, and tell it to take a hike!

Fear becomes our enemy and it's something we typically fight with. Fear sets in to destroy and can be catastrophic to a marriage. Typically, when you are sitting in fear, you are terrified and often feel panicked. For example, have you ever felt lonely in your relationship? You know your husband is physically there, but the disconnection is so deep that you feel alone. When fear begins to set in, you become resistant to it and your instinct is to fight the fear. Your fear starts causing you to have negative thoughts. As the loneliness grows, the fear of your husband leaving starts to increase, and as a result, you begin to have anxiety and worry. Your mind is now being controlled by fear, and that leads to one negative thought after another. The longer you hold on to the fear or try to push it away, the worse it gets. Often, you will lash out at your husband and he has no idea why. His defense mechanisms quickly go up, and the next thing you know you are at war with him. Therefore, it is imperative to acknowledge fear when it arrives. By not acknowledging it you are risking disastrous outcomes in your marriage. You have to take a step back and determine what is causing the fear. Decipher the facts and feelings. Once you have sorted through this, you simply ask it to leave

I am so grateful for Dack Quigley for creating The First Class Seminar because that seminar brought me back to life! It gave me the courage to pursue my dreams and to overcome a relationship I thought was headed toward divorce. For God's sake, I wrote a book because I was able to let go of the fear!

Chapter 13:

Don't Let the Roadblocks
Stop You

My nineteen-year-old daughter recently applied to a university to pursue her dream career. The admissions office called her and informed her that her high school graduating GPA was lower than the required standards. They asked her to write a letter explaining any hardships she faced that caused her grades to be less than what they required. She was determined to get accepted, so she set out to write her letter. She found herself feeling frustrated and called me to talk through it.

She said to me, "Mom, I feel like this is just a letter of excuses. I could tell them a million things I went through that caused me not to focus on my grades. They were all things that really happened and stuff that I went through, but at the end of the day, they are just excuses. I chose not to make school a priority. I chose not to study harder. I chose not to get up and go to school. Regardless of whatever justification I come up with, they are ultimately just excuses."

I responded with, "Ok, so what are you going to do about it? What are you risking by not trying to get into the university, and what happens if you don't take any action and just give up?"

Without hesitation she said, "I'm going to do what you have always taught me; I'm going to own up to my faults. I'm going to tell them that I chose not to make school a priority, and any event or situation I tell you about is simply an excuse. What I did in my past doesn't matter because what matters is what I am doing now." This may have been one of my proudest mom moments ever. She wrote the letter, owned up to her faults, and got accepted into the university.

Ask yourself what you are risking by not making a change in your marriage, and what will happen if you don't take action? I know you want to make a change, or you wouldn't still be reading this book. Is it going to be easy? No. But is the alternative more painful? I don't know, only you can answer that. What I do know is that when you walk yourself through each step, you will be able to transform your marriage from broken to beautiful! I highly recommend that you seek out support. Asking for guidance doesn't mean you are weak, it means you are *brilliant!* If you want someone to hold your hand through these steps, then contact me and I will be right there with you as you travel through this journey. Send me an email to get started and don't wait! Waiting delays your happiness so choose you now!

By now, either your head is spinning, or you have clear direction about what your next move is. Just know that there will be a million things that will come up and try to get in your way of working to create your desired marriage. But at the end of the day, these are just excuses. There will always be reasons why you can't do something, or excuses not to choose differently. Roadblocks will appear out of nowhere and life will always happen. If you can't do it alone and need guidance to push you along, then ask for help. Ask me, I can help you help yourself! If you can tackle it on your own, then congratulations, and get to it! Use whatever mechanism you need to make the change but know that as long as you have one-hundred percent intention to create your dream marriage, then you will get there.

Chapter 14:

Bursting into Beautiful

People will always try to destroy your dreams. Don't let them. Just keep building and working toward achieving them! The old quote, "If you dream it, you can achieve it," is so powerful and so true. Don't let others cloud your vision. If you want a marriage that is filled with love, communication, and true joy, then envision it, believe it, and make it happen.

Remember to always be mindful of how past experiences can affect not only yourself but your spouse too. Love with more compassion and understanding and watch how your relationship will transform. If you can put your judgement aside and acknowledge that perhaps he is responding based on something that has nothing to do with you, you will learn to love him in a different way. And when you love him through those hard times and don't take them personally, he will love you back. So don't forget that experiences do affect you!

I challenge you to start asking for what you want and know that this is not selfish. That is just a limiting belief that you are telling yourself. You will remove the gray area if you are willing to freely ask for what you want. It's hard, yes, no one here will deny that. Your communication with your husband will drastically improve if you are willing to just ask. As a result, you won't leave him wondering! Be clear, concise, and ask for what you want!

Your limiting beliefs will never stop creeping in. Tell them to go away, scream at them, write them down, then throw them away. Stop believing all the bull crap you are making up in your head. Kick the limiting beliefs to the curb or chuck them in the suck-it bucket and move on!

Life is all about choices. Perhaps this is another cliché, but it is the truth. You are the only one responsible for your happiness, and you cannot depend on someone else for it. You have to set out to apply effort in creating your own happiness and fight through the things that will try to stop you. Your husband cannot make you happy, you are the only one who can do that because happiness is a choice and only you can choose it!

Loving yourself is vital to creating a happy marriage. If you do not love yourself, then he cannot love you either. When you fall in love with yourself, he will fall in love with you too. Make time to do what makes you feel fulfilled and create a relationship with yourself. If you have to, stand in front of the mirror every day and say, I love myself!

One of the greatest ways to love yourself is to find forgiveness, not only in others but also in yourself. Your husband wants to be forgiven just as much as you want to be forgiven. It's OK to feel your emotions, so sort through them, experience them, accept things for what they are, and move on. Holding on to hatred, hurt, and grudges does not serve you. Give yourself some grace, give it to others, and stop beating yourself up. Remember that forgiveness is a necessity!

Learn from all experiences and take time to reflect after the storm. Everything happens for a reason and lessons are waiting to be discovered. Don't dwell about what isn't. Instead, search for the unanswered prayers, because they are waiting for you.

Fear will creep into your marriage appearing as something else because it's a sneaky little devil. Acknowledge it when it is happening, identify what's causing it, and kick it to the curb. Fear will destroy everything in its path, including your marriage, so it must be managed. Release it and let go of the fear!

I firmly believe that by applying these revelations to my life saved my marriage, and I know that if you do the same, a transformation will occur. You will find the confidence to pursue your dream come true of having a joyful marriage. One where you can effectively communicate with your husband again and bring back the spark. I hope you discover your self-worth and understand the value in making these changes. I'm very clear as to why I am here and why I figured this out. It was to help others discover that they already possess what they need to achieve their happily ever after and all I have to do is show them. I will not stop fighting for women, to help them see what I see, because you're important and you matter and so does your happiness. Don't give up on yourself and don't be afraid to seek out support. I am proud of you for choosing you! Apply what you have learned and watch your marriage transform from broken to beautiful!

Acknowledgments

For twenty years, I had a dream of writing a book. What was stopping me? Belief. I simply made a choice to believe I had what it took to be an author. I attended a personal growth seminar and magically shifted my mindset that made my dream a reality. For that, I want to thank Susan Grateke for encouraging me to attend The First Class and Dack Quigley for teaching and mentoring me in a way that pushed me to make that shift. Dack—Thank you for your encouragement and belief and more importantly, for reminding me that I am always a student.

Big Dave—you are a true inspiration and I am so grateful for your friendship and guidance. Thank you for your willingness to share and help open my eyes to new possibilities. You are a wise man and I am grateful to call you my friend.

I want to thank my mom for teaching me to be generous and to my dad for teaching me to love all mankind. These are gifts you both gave me that I will forever be grateful for them.

Thank you to my children, you are my greatest blessing and I am so grateful I get to be your mom.

Thank you to my dear friend and assistant, Natasha Fisher. You held me up through all the blood, sweat and tears to ensure this book was completed. Your ability to push me through some of the toughest times means more to me than words can express.

Last but not least, to my husband Joe, my gratitude for you is infinite. Thank you for sticking by my side through some of our darkest moments. Your unconditional love and support have helped push me through things I never dreamed possible. Thank you for reminding me just how beautiful I truly am. Thank you for being my best friend, I truly love you with all my heart.

Thank you to Angela Lauria and The Author Incubator's team, as well as to David Hancock and the Morgan James Publishing team for helping me bring this book to print.

Thank You

Thank you for reading my book! I hope you found these steps to be helpful and that you're able to apply them to your relationship. Sometimes it is helpful to have someone walk through them with you. Having your own personal cheerleader can better assist you with achieving greater success when implementing these steps into your life. If that is something you feel would help you and you want my personal help doing so, then reach out to me for more information on how to get started. I am committed to helping you get the best results that will transform your marriage and I look forward to watching your life go from *broken to beautiful.*

For more information you can email me at:
sarahjane@lifecoachsarahjane.com

About the Author

Sarah Jane Patton is the author of *From Broken to Beautiful: 9 Secrets That Will Transform Your Marriage*. She coaches women who are struggling with their relationships by helping them discover their self-worth and focus on self-love. Sarah has a passion for helping women in need and is committed to continuing her work in personal development. She is the founder of the OLSON Foundation, a not for profit organization that provides funding for women in need. She resides just outside of St. Louis, Missouri, with her husband and eight children.